AF228594

INSIDE THE NBA

PHILADELPHIA 76ERS

BY PATRICK DONNELLY

SportsZone

An Imprint of Abdo Publishing
abdobooks.com

abdobooks.com

Published by Abdo Publishing, a division of ABDO, PO Box 398166, Minneapolis, Minnesota 55439. Copyright © 2023 by Abdo Consulting Group, Inc. International copyrights reserved in all countries. No part of this book may be reproduced in any form without written permission from the publisher. SportsZone™ is a trademark and logo of Abdo Publishing.

Printed in China
052022
092022

Cover Photo: Matt Slocum/AP Images
Interior Photos: Melinda Nagy/Shutterstock Images, 1; Drew Hallowell/Getty Images Sport/Getty Images, 4, 33; Kyle Ross/Icon Sportswire/Getty Images, 7; Mitchell Leff/Getty Images Sport/Getty Images, 8, 9, 11, 23; AP Images, 12, 24; Bettmann/Getty Images, 14; Focus on Sport/Getty Images, 17, 19, 27, 28, 34, 37, 38; Sporting News/Getty Images, 20; Al Messerschmidt/AP Images, 30; Ezra Shaw/Getty Images Sport/Getty Images, 31; Tom Mihalek/AFP/Getty Images, 39; Jed Jacobsohn/Allsport/Getty Images Sport/Getty Images, 41

Editor: Charlie Beattie
Series Designer: Joshua Olson

Library of Congress Control Number: 2021951667

Publisher's Cataloging-in-Publication Data

Names: Donnelly, Patrick, author.
Title: Philadelphia 76ers / by Patrick Donnelly
Description: Minneapolis, Minnesota: Abdo Publishing, 2023 | Series: Inside the NBA | Includes online resources and index.
Identifiers: ISBN 9781532198403 (lib. bdg.) | ISBN 9781098272050 (ebook)
Subjects: LCSH: Philadelphia 76ers (Basketball team)--Juvenile literature. | Basketball--Juvenile literature. | Professional sports--Juvenile literature. | Sports franchises--Juvenile literature.
Classification: DDC 796.32364--dc23

TABLE OF CONTENTS

WE'RE ALL GAMERS.

CHAPTER ONE

STREAKING 76ERS

The fans at Philadelphia's Wells Fargo Center went silent when they saw Joel Embiid fall to the floor. Their team was on a roll. The National Basketball Association (NBA) playoffs were in sight. But now their star was down and injured. Philadelphia supporters could see their championship dreams disappearing before their eyes.

The 76ers were one of the NBA's most exciting teams during the 2017–18 season. Embiid had emerged as one of the league's most promising young stars. The 24-year-old center made his first All-Star Game appearance that February. He was leading the 76ers in scoring, rebounding, and blocked shots. The team was on a roll. The 76ers had won seven straight heading into their game against the New York Knicks on March 28, 2018.

Early in the second quarter, Embiid had the ball at the top of the three-point circle. He went to hand it to rookie

Led by young center Joel Embiid, the 76ers surged to the playoffs in 2017–18.

guard Markelle Fultz. The 7-foot Embiid bent down to meet Fultz while shielding the ball from a Knicks defender. As Fultz grabbed the ball, his shoulder smashed into the left side of Embiid's face. The big man dropped to the floor.

Embiid was taken to a local hospital to test for a possible concussion. But the news turned out to be even worse. Embiid had broken an orbital bone around his left eye. Doctors said he could be sidelined for up to a month as he recovered.

The 76ers went on to defeat the Knicks. Their winning streak stretched to eight games. It was Philadelphia's best run since 2003. This was unfamiliar territory for the 76ers. Just two years earlier, they had won only 10 games in an entire season. Now they were making a playoff push. The victory over the Knicks moved them into fourth place in the Eastern Conference. But with eight games remaining in the season, the 76ers were suddenly missing their star center. Fans wondered if the team could survive without him.

A LONG ROAD BACK

Five months earlier, the season had begun with high hopes in Philadelphia. The team hadn't made the playoffs in six years. Their 10–72 finish in 2015–16 was the third-worst season of any team in NBA history. But a sense of optimism was bubbling beneath the surface. Much of that was due to Embiid.

Embiid is tended to by team doctors after colliding with teammate Markelle Fultz against the New York Knicks in March 2018.

He had been the third overall pick of the 2014 NBA Draft. However, due to a foot injury, he didn't actually debut until 2016–17. He proved to be worth the wait. Though the 76ers limited his minutes, Embiid still averaged 20.2 points, 7.8 rebounds, and 2.5 blocks per game.

It wasn't all perfect. Embiid suffered a torn meniscus in his left knee and missed the second half of the season. But when he played, the 76ers were a better team. It wasn't hard to imagine how much better they would be with Embiid playing a full season.

After sitting out his first two NBA seasons with foot injuries, Embiid finally debuted for the 76ers in 2016–17.

RESILIENCE ON DISPLAY

The 76ers were hovering around .500 in December 2017 but then suffered a stretch of nine losses in 10 games. It looked like another Philadelphia season was about to fizzle out.

However, these were not the same old 76ers. Rookie point guard Ben Simmons was a triple-double threat every time he walked onto the court. Veteran guard J. J. Redick was an elite three-point shooter. Versatile forwards Robert Covington and Dario Šarić gave Philadelphia a little bit of everything. And Embiid was in All-Star form.

The 76ers righted the ship after their December skid with a 9–2 stretch. Then they won eight of nine games to start February. That run moved them into the seventh spot in the Eastern Conference with a 32–25 record.

These 76ers weren't going to be satisfied with just slipping into the

In Embiid's absence, players like Dario Šarić stepped up to keep Philadelphia's winning streak alive.

playoffs, however. On March 15, they beat the Knicks in New York 118–110. Embiid had 29 points, and Simmons posted a triple-double of 13 points, 12 assists, and 10 rebounds.

That proved to be the start of something big. Next, they swept a three-game homestand against the Brooklyn Nets, Charlotte Hornets, and Memphis Grizzlies. They beat the Magic by 20 in Orlando. Then came three more wins at home, against the Minnesota Timberwolves, Denver Nuggets, and Knicks. However, it was in that Knicks victory that Embiid was injured.

The 76ers needed other players to step up. And that's exactly what happened. It seemed like a new hero emerged every game. Forward Ersan İlyasova came off the bench to score 21 points and grab 16 rebounds in a 10-point win over the Atlanta Hawks. Then reserve guard Marco Belinelli scored a game-high 22 points against Charlotte. The 119–102 victory was Philadelphia's tenth straight. Two nights later, eight 76ers posted double-digit points in a 121–95 rout of the Nets.

Philadelphia's biggest challenge arrived on April 6. LeBron James and the defending Eastern Conference champion Cleveland Cavaliers came to town. The 76ers showed no fear. They raced out to a 30-point lead in the second quarter. James almost brought the Cavs back, scoring 44 points along with 11 rebounds and 11 assists. But Simmons posted a triple-double of his own with 27 points, 15 rebounds, and 13 assists. Cavaliers forward Larry Nance Jr.

Ben Simmons skies for a dunk against the Cleveland Cavaliers on April 6, 2018.

missed a layup attempt at the buzzer. The 76ers held on for a 132–130 win.

They finished out the season with three more wins, including a 130–95 laugher over the Milwaukee Bucks. That ran the streak to 16, a franchise record.

The 76ers had completed their franchise turnaround in style. The 10-win season was now a distant memory. Their 52–30 record earned them the number three seed in the Eastern Conference playoffs. And the winning streak showed that the team had the depth and the heart to compete, even with their All-Star center on the sidelines.

CHAPTER TWO

NATIONALS TO 76ERS

The National Basketball League (NBL) began long before the NBA. The league's first games were played in the mid-1930s. By 1946 the league had caught the eye of Danny Biasone. He had arrived in the United States from Italy as an 11-year-old in 1920. In the 1940s, he owned a bowling alley in Syracuse, New York. At that time, the nearby Rochester Royals were a successful team. Biasone saw that and wanted his own team in Syracuse. He paid $5,000 to enter the league.

The Nationals played in the final three years of the NBL's existence. In 1949 the NBL merged with the Basketball Association of America to form the NBA. The Nationals were one of seven NBL teams to join the new league.

Syracuse was a hit right out of the gate. The Nationals won 16 of their first 17 games. They cruised to the Eastern Division title with a 51–13 record. Syracuse's star was 21-year-old center

Al Cervi played for the Nationals during their first four NBA seasons, and he coached the team until 1957.

Dolph Schayes. He was the NBL's Rookie of the Year in its final season. The next year, he led the Nationals in scoring at 16.8 points per game. Meanwhile, player/coach Al Cervi ran the show as the team's point guard. The Nationals reached the first NBA Finals but lost to the Minneapolis Lakers in six games.

After losing again to the Lakers in 1954, the Nationals returned to the Finals in 1955. This time they came out victorious over the Fort Wayne Pistons in a seven-game thriller.

Nationals guard George King, *left*, battles for a loose ball against Bob Cousy of the Boston Celtics.

Guard George King sealed the victory in Game 7. First, he hit a free throw with 12 seconds left to break a 91–91 tie. King then stole the ball from Fort Wayne guard Andy Phillip on the Pistons' last possession.

That was the high-water mark for the Nationals. Though they made the playoffs in all 14 of their NBA seasons, they never again advanced past the division finals.

WINDS OF CHANGE

The NBA underwent major changes as the 1950s marched on. Teams moved to bigger cities where they could make more money. The Lakers became the first NBA team in California in 1960. Two years later, the Philadelphia Warriors were sold to a group that moved the team to San Francisco.

Philadelphia was too big a basketball market to go without a team for long. And Biasone was losing money in Syracuse. He decided to sell the Nationals. A group from Philadelphia stepped up. They bought the team and moved it south in time to start the 1963–64 season.

The team was quickly renamed the 76ers. Schayes was now the coach, though he also played in 24 games before retiring at the end of the season. Guard Hal Greer led the team in scoring at 23.3 points per game. Two other players—veteran center Red Kerr and second-year forward Chet Walker—averaged double-doubles as Philadelphia reached the playoffs.

WINNING WITH WILT

Wilt Chamberlain was a Philadelphia native. The towering center had also been the NBA's leading star early in his career with the Philadelphia Warriors. Chamberlain moved with the team to San Francisco in 1962. He was still at the top of his game in January 1965 when the Warriors decided to trade him.

Meanwhile, the 76ers had begun playing in Philadelphia. Fans there were thrilled when the team sent three players to San Francisco for Chamberlain. He was the superstar who could push the team over the top. But his return didn't provide an instant spark for the 76ers. They were hovering around .500 at the time of the trade and finished the season 40–40.

In the playoffs, Philadelphia proved it could be dangerous. Chamberlain led the team on a deep run. The 76ers knocked off the Cincinnati Royals in the first round. Then they took the eventual-champion Boston Celtics to seven games before falling in the Eastern Division finals. That set the stage for 1966–67. Chamberlain won his second straight Most Valuable Player (MVP) Award, and Philadelphia won a league-record 68 games. They met the Celtics again in the Eastern Division finals. This time, the 76ers dominated, taking the series in five games. Then they beat the Warriors—Philadelphia's old team— in six games in the Finals.

That was the peak for the 76ers and Chamberlain, who was traded to the Lakers in July 1968. That began a big slide for

Superstar Wilt Chamberlain (13) and the 76ers finally topped the mighty Boston Celtics on their way to winning the 1967 NBA title.

the 76ers, who bottomed out in 1972–73 with a 9–73 record. But they made a quick turnaround. Just three years after posting the worst record in NBA history, they were back in the playoffs. And then they acquired one of the game's brightest stars. In 1976 Philadelphia purchased the contract of Julius "Dr. J" Erving from the New York Nets.

Erving led the 76ers to a division title and the NBA Finals in his first season. But the Portland Trail Blazers rallied from a 2–0 deficit to win four straight games. Erving and the 76ers missed out on a championship ring.

That became a familiar story over the next few seasons. Erving continued to shine. But his supporting cast was not quite good enough to win it all. In the next five years, the 76ers lost in the conference finals twice and in the NBA Finals twice.

Once again, a trade for an All-Star center helped put them over the top. This time, they acquired Moses Malone from the Houston Rockets in 1982. He was the league's reigning MVP. Malone led the 76ers in scoring and the NBA in rebounding to win his second straight MVP honor.

After the 76ers posted the league's best record in 1982–83, Malone predicted they would sweep every playoff game. They nearly did, winning the NBA title with only one postseason loss. A sweep of Los Angeles in the Finals avenged two previous losses to the Lakers.

THE ANSWER

Erving retired after the 1987 playoffs. But the 76ers already had another forward ready to assume a leadership role. Charles Barkley took over from Erving as the team's most recognizable name. However, he never delivered playoff success. The 76ers

Charles Barkley emerged as the 76ers' primary offensive weapon in the late 1980s.

didn't even make it to the playoffs in 1987–88, their first year without Dr. J.

Even with Barkley as one of the league's best rebounders and scorers, Philadelphia could not get past the second playoff round. It got even worse when Barkley was traded to the Phoenix Suns in 1992. None of the three players who came back in the deal stuck around very long. Philadelphia dropped out of the playoffs for seven straight years.

Allen Iverson attacks the basket against the Charlotte Hornets.

With the team officially in rebuilding mode, success on the court was hard to come by. After the 76ers went 18–64 in 1995–96, they had the best chance at nabbing the top pick in the NBA Draft Lottery. And when the lottery balls fell their way, they had the first choice in a deep and talented draft.

The 76ers selected Georgetown University point guard Allen Iverson with their top pick. Known as "the Answer," he certainly was that for Philadelphia. He led the NBA in scoring and led the 76ers to the playoffs in his third season. In 2000–01 Iverson won his second scoring title as Philadelphia finished 56–26. Iverson was named NBA MVP. The 76ers won their first division title since 1990 and had the top seed in the Eastern Conference Playoffs. Iverson led them on a thrilling run to the NBA Finals. There they lost in five games to a new Lakers powerhouse.

Iverson stuck around for five more years but failed to recapture the glory of that 2001 playoff run. And when he was traded to the Denver Nuggets in 2006, the 76ers fell back to the middle of the pack in the NBA. They made the playoffs four times in the next six years but won just one series.

THE PROCESS

Philadelphia's management decided in 2013 that if they weren't going to be good, they might as well get *really* bad. They began stripping the roster, trading veteran players for future draft picks. The 76ers lost games at a historic pace so those selections would be more valuable.

Fans were frustrated, but team general manager Sam Hinkie urged them to "trust the process." However, many people thought the process was nothing more than the 76ers losing on purpose. Hinkie was mocked frequently around the league. It got worse when Philadelphia lost 26 straight games in February and March 2014. "The Process" was the talk of the season when the 76ers won only 10 games two years later.

Hinkie's process extended longer than planned because two of his top picks—center Joel Embiid and guard Ben Simmons—missed a combined three seasons due to injuries. Once they joined the active roster, the 76ers began to thrive. The team began a new playoff streak by winning 52 games in 2017–18.

The 76ers were officially back on top in 2020–21. They won 49 games and finished first in the Eastern Conference. But after a shocking loss to the Atlanta Hawks in the second round of the playoffs, changes were needed. After sitting out for several months, Simmons was traded to the Nets in February 2022. In return, the 76ers received former MVP James Harden. The 32-year-old guard clicked with Embiid initially. But Harden's play fell off in the playoffs as Philadelphia was again eliminated in the second round.

However, a young star guard emerged for Philadelphia during the 2021–22 season. Guard Tyrese Maxey was Philadelphia's first-round pick in 2020. After playing little as a rookie, he became an exciting starter in his second season. As the team looked for another star to pair with Embiid, fans in Philadelphia hoped the 21-year-old Maxey was finally the answer.

Tyrese Maxey averaged 17.5 points and 4.3 assists for the 76ers in 2021–22.

Nats
4
PHILADELPHIA

CHAPTER THREE

PHILLY'S FINEST

The Nationals probably wouldn't have survived in Syracuse as long as they did without the play of Dolph Schayes. The 6-foot-8-inch forward was one of the NBA's first stars. Schayes was among the league's most consistent scorers and rebounders. He grabbed more than 12 rebounds per game for 11 straight seasons. And he was the league's all-time leading scorer when he retired. The 12-time All-Star made the move to Philadelphia and served as player-coach for the 76ers' first season.

Before that, Schayes was the centerpiece of Syracuse's 1955 NBA champions. He averaged a double-double in the finals against the Fort Wayne Pistons. Red Kerr also put up big numbers against Fort Wayne. The 22-year-old center was at the start of a long career in a Syracuse/Philadelphia uniform.

Dolph Schayes (4) played the first 14 seasons of his career in Syracuse and his final year in Philadelphia after the franchise became the 76ers in 1963.

On the Clock

Danny Biasone was more than just the owner of the Nationals. He helped create one of the game's most important innovations, the 24-second shot clock. In the NBA's early days, teams often employed stall tactics to keep the ball away from the game's dominant big men. Biasone knew fans wanted to see players shoot, not stand around holding the ball. He studied box scores and determined the ideal number of shots each team would take in a fast-paced game. Biasone then used that total to set the clock at 24 seconds. The NBA added it in 1954, and it was an instant hit.

When he finally left in 1965, only Schayes had more points in franchise history.

In 1958 the Nationals used a second-round draft pick on guard Hal Greer from Marshall University in West Virginia. Greer didn't think he had a chance in the league. He didn't even unpack when he got to Syracuse.

Instead of failing, Greer was the first piece to Philadelphia's next championship puzzle. He was a double-digit scorer from his first season. And when the 76ers won the title in 1967, Greer averaged 27.7 points in 15 playoff games. When he retired in 1973, Greer had played 1,122 career games, the most in team history.

The 1967 NBA title was a crowning moment for Wilt Chamberlain. The superstar center entered the league with the Philadelphia Warriors in 1959. From his first day, he put up amazing scoring and rebounding numbers. He even scored 100 points in a single game in 1962.

But Chamberlain kept coming up short of a championship. Finally, alongside Greer and sharpshooter Billy Cunningham, Chamberlain and the 76ers got over the hump.

THE GOOD DOCTOR

Julius "Dr. J" Erving was just 26 years old when he joined the 76ers in 1976. But he was already a veteran of five seasons in the American Basketball Association (ABA). Erving's New York Nets won that rival league's title in 1976. He made the jump to the NBA when the leagues merged that summer. But the Nets' finances were a mess. They needed cash to survive, so the 76ers stepped up and purchased Erving's contract for $6 million. Half of that went to the Nets, and the other half went to Erving.

Few athletes have ever been more closely associated with Philadelphia than Erving. Fans around the league flocked to arenas to watch "the Doctor" operate. Whether it was a soaring

Billy Cunningham helped the 76ers win an NBA title as a player in 1967, then coached the team to another championship in 1983.

Julius Erving (6) retired as the 76ers' third all-time leading scorer.

dunk, a silky jumper, or a graceful move to score in traffic, he usually sent fans home happy.

Erving won just one NBA title in his career. That came with the dominant 1982–83 76ers. By then he had help from one of the game's most dominant big men. The championship 76ers revolved around Moses Malone. Philadelphia traded for him in September 1982. Malone was coming off an MVP season with the Houston Rockets. Thick-bodied and tenacious, he was a terror in the low post. He won six NBA rebounding titles, including three in four years with the 76ers. And he scored more than 20 points per game in 11 straight seasons.

While Erving and Malone manned the frontcourt, a pair of guards did most of the work on the outside. Andrew Toney was a threat to score from all over the floor. His deadly jump shooting helped him average 19.7 points per game that year. And point guard Maurice Cheeks was a defensive ace who averaged 6.9 assists and made his first All-Star appearance.

TALKING THE TALK

Charles Barkley was brash and loud. He also dominated on the court. The fifth pick of the 1984 NBA Draft spent his first eight seasons in Philadelphia. Barkley averaged at least 20 points and 10 rebounds seven times in eight years with the 76ers. Nicknamed "the Round Mound of Rebound," the stocky Barkley was generously listed at 6-foot-6. But he used every inch

Look Out Below!

Nobody would ever dispute that Darryl Dawkins was a character. The 6-foot-11-inch center played for the 76ers from 1975 to 1982. He liked to say he was an alien from Planet Lovetron. And he lived up to his nickname, Chocolate Thunder, with his ferocious dunks. In 1979 he twice shattered backboards with powerful slams. The NBA then instituted "the Dawkins Rule," banning players from hanging on the rim.

Charles Barkley throws down a dunk against the Miami Heat in 1991.

of his height and bulk to clear space under the hoop. He also had surprising agility to get to loose balls.

The franchise's next big star was often the smallest player on the court. Allen Iverson was just 6 feet tall and weighed 160 pounds. But he was fearless. Iverson joined the team as a rookie in 1996. From the start, Iverson showed he wasn't afraid to put his body on the line to win the game.

He's often been described as "pound for pound" the toughest player in NBA history. Iverson took the ball to the hoop without worrying about the bruising defenders in his way. But for all the contact he drew, he was amazingly durable. Iverson led the NBA in minutes played seven times, including five of his 12 seasons with the 76ers.

Allen Iverson averaged a career-high 33.0 points per game during his final full season with the 76ers in 2005–06.

The 1997 NBA Rookie of the Year and 2001 NBA MVP won four league scoring titles. He entered the Basketball Hall of Fame in 2016.

Iverson led the 76ers back to the NBA Finals in 2001. The 76ers' feisty guard led the league in scoring at 31.1 points per game. He also averaged a league-best 2.5 steals per contest. The Philadelphia offense was a bit lopsided. No other player scored more than 12.4 points per game that season. But veteran center Dikembe Mutombo, acquired at the trading deadline, provided rebounding and a shot-blocking presence on defense. And steady guard Eric Snow ran the show when the ball wasn't in Iverson's hands.

THE PROCESS BEARS FRUIT

Joel Embiid was the third overall pick of the 2014 NBA Draft. Two years later, Philadelphia landed Ben Simmons with the draft's top pick. They both struggled with injuries early in their careers. Embiid missed his first two seasons due to a broken bone in his foot. Simmons, meanwhile, rolled his ankle during training camp his rookie year. X-rays later revealed a broken bone in his foot that sidelined him for a full season.

Once they finally got on the court, both players displayed the skills that had made them such valuable draft picks. Embiid proved equally effective near the hoop and beyond the three-point arc. And his shot-blocking skills helped disrupt opposing offenses. Simmons ran the Philadelphia offense while also earning All-Defensive First Team honors in 2020 and 2021. But Simmons became increasingly reluctant to shoot as his career went on. After the team's playoff loss to Atlanta in 2021, the young guard was traded away. Meanwhile, Embiid's star rose even higher in 2021–22. He averaged an NBA-best 30.6 points per game. Embiid was the first center to top the NBA in scoring since 1999–2000.

Joel Embiid's combination of inside skills and an effective jump shot makes him one of the NBA's toughest players to guard.

CHAPTER FOUR

STARS EARN THEIR STRIPES

In 1965 the 76ers were still looking to make a name for themselves in their new city. They needed a big splash, and they found just the right guy to make it. Philadelphia native Wilt Chamberlain was a hometown hero who had moved west when the Warriors relocated to San Francisco. The 76ers brought him back in a January trade. And his impact became obvious his first postseason with his new team. Chamberlain, who'd just won his sixth straight NBA scoring title, teamed with Hal Greer and Chet Walker to knock off Cincinnati three games to one in the first round. Chamberlain scored 38 points and grabbed 26 boards in the clincher.

That set up an Eastern Division finals series against Boston. The Celtics had won six straight NBA titles and posted a league-high 62 wins that season. Chamberlain resumed his legendary rivalry with Celtics center Bill Russell. Greer and

Wilt Chamberlain averaged 21.6 points and 32.0 rebounds per game in Philadelphia's five-game win over the Boston Celtics in the 1967 Eastern Division finals.

Walker gave the Celtics fits as the 76ers took them the distance. But a last-second steal preserved Boston's one-point victory in Game 7.

The next season, the 76ers won the Eastern Division over Boston for the first time in a decade. But the Celtics had the last laugh again, beating Philadelphia in five games in the Eastern Division finals.

Still, the 76ers had proved they could compete with Boston. And in 1966–67, Philadelphia knocked the Celtics from their throne. Philadelphia raced out of the gate, winning 46 of their first 50 games. The 76ers finished 68–13, the best record in NBA history at that point. But they had gone just 4–5 against the Celtics in the regular season.

The playoff matchup was a different story. Philadelphia won the first three against Boston in the Eastern Division finals. The Celtics won Game 4 by four points to prevent a sweep. But back in Philadelphia, the 76ers would not be denied. Chamberlain carried the team on his back, finishing with 29 points, 36 rebounds, and 13 assists as the 76ers rolled 140–116.

The NBA Finals brought a matchup with Philadelphia's old team, now the San Francisco Warriors. Even with the NBA's leading scorer, Rick Barry, the Warriors were no match for the 76ers. Barry averaged 40.8 points per game. But Philadelphia took home the title in six games. The 76ers won Game 6 on the

Julius Erving won his only NBA title in 1983.

road to clinch their first title since 1955, when they were still the Syracuse Nationals.

"FO, FO, FO"

The 76ers returned to the NBA Finals in 1977, Julius Erving's first season in Philadelphia. They fell short of winning it all, even after taking a 2–0 lead in the Finals. Center Bill Walton led the Portland Trail Blazers to four straight victories. A handful of close calls in the next five years showed that Erving needed a bit more help to put the 76ers over the top.

That help arrived in the fall of 1982, when Philadelphia acquired NBA MVP Moses Malone from Houston. Malone wasn't

Moses Malone was named NBA Finals MVP in 1983 after averaging 25.8 points and 18.0 rebounds in a four-game sweep of the Los Angeles Lakers.

one to talk a lot. He let his play on the court speak for him. And it spoke volumes as he won a second straight MVP Award and the 76ers won a league-best 65 games.

Malone's quiet confidence spread throughout the locker room as the season played out. But just before the playoffs began, Malone spoke up. He was asked how he thought the 76ers would fare in the playoffs. His response will be remembered in Philadelphia forever.

In his thick Virginia drawl, Malone replied, "Fo, fo, fo"— meaning the 76ers would win each series in four games.

"Fo, fo, fo" became a rallying cry of sorts as the 76ers cruised through the playoffs.

Malone's prediction was nearly 100 percent correct. Philadelphia's only loss came in Game 4 of the Eastern Conference finals at Milwaukee. The 76ers followed that up by sweeping the defending-champion Los Angeles Lakers.

AI TO THE RESCUE

Behind Michael Jordan, the Chicago Bulls won six NBA championships in the 1990s. Jordan left the team for good in 1998. That meant the Eastern Conference was once again anyone's to win. And in 2001, after the New York Knicks and Indiana Pacers had each won the crown, the 76ers decided it was their turn.

The 76ers earned the top seed in the East with a 56–26 record. They opened the playoffs by

Philadelphia center Dikembe Mutombo salutes after the 76ers knocked off the Milwaukee Bucks to reach the 2001 NBA Finals.

taking down the Pacers in four games. Their second-round series against Toronto was an epic battle between Iverson and Raptors guard Vince Carter. Iverson topped 50 points twice. Carter averaged 30.4 points in the series. Iverson got his teammates involved in Game 7 with 16 assists. Still, it took a final miss from Carter to let the 76ers escape with a one-point victory.

Philadelphia survived another seven-game thriller in the Eastern Conference finals against the Milwaukee Bucks. This time Game 7 was a classic Iverson performance as he finished with 44 points. Center Dikembe Mutombo added 23 points, 19 rebounds, and seven blocks. Philadelphia ran away late to win 108–91.

Iverson was back at it again in Game 1 of the Finals against the Lakers. Few gave Philadelphia a chance against the team led by center Shaquille O'Neal and guard Kobe Bryant. The Lakers had won 19 straight games, including all 11 of their playoff contests. But Philadelphia had the ultimate underdog in Iverson.

The teams dueled into overtime in Game 1. Throughout the game, Lakers guard Tyronn Lue had been playing physical defense with Iverson. But with 1:19 left, the 76ers star hit a three-pointer to put Philadelphia up 101–99. After a Lakers turnover, the 76ers had a chance to finish off the upset.

Iverson caught a pass from guard Aaron McKie on the wing. Then he dribbled to the corner and squared up to Lue. Iverson took a quick jab step and dropped back for a fadeaway jumper. As Lue lunged out to challenge the shot, he stumbled and fell. After the bucket dropped in, Iverson stared down at Lue, then calmly stepped over his beaten opponent. The 76ers went on to win the game.

Allen Iverson averaged 32.6 points, 6.1 assists, and 2.4 steals during the 2001 NBA playoffs.

The Lakers took the next four to claim the NBA crown. But Iverson's shot and icy celebration became the lasting memory of the series.

TIMELINE

1946

Bowling alley owner Danny Biasone sends a $5,000 check to the NBL offices, and the Syracuse Nationals are born.

1950

The Nationals finish their first NBA season 51–13 and reach the Finals before losing to the Minneapolis Lakers in six games.

1954

The NBA adopts the 24-second shot clock, thanks to the suggestion of Biasone.

1955

The Nationals win their only title in Syracuse, taking down the Fort Wayne Pistons in seven games.

1963

Biasone sells the Nationals, and the team moves to Philadelphia, where it is renamed the 76ers.

1967

After losing to Boston in two straight Eastern Division finals, the 76ers finally get past the Celtics, then defeat the San Francisco Warriors to win the NBA title. Their 68 regular-season wins were an NBA record at the time.

1973

The 76ers finish 9–73, a mark that remains the worst for a full season in NBA history.

1977

Behind superstar forward Julius "Dr. J" Erving, the 76ers reach the NBA Finals and take a two-game lead before falling to the Portland Trail Blazers.

1982

Philadelphia loses to the Los Angeles Lakers in the NBA Finals for the second time in three years, prompting the team to trade for Houston Rockets center Moses Malone.

1983

Behind Malone's second straight MVP season, the 76ers storm through the regular season and playoffs to win their first NBA championship in 16 years.

1992

The 76ers trade All-Star forward Charles Barkley to the Phoenix Suns.

1996

Philadelphia wins the NBA Draft Lottery and uses the first pick to select Georgetown University guard Allen Iverson.

2001

Iverson wins his second NBA scoring title and is named the league MVP before leading the 76ers to the NBA Finals, where they fall to the Lakers in five games.

2013

The 76ers begin "the Process," stripping their roster of veterans in hopes of losing to acquire higher draft picks. The strategy pays off with the future selections of center Joel Embiid and guard Ben Simmons.

2018

The 76ers end the season on a 16-game winning streak and defeat the Miami Heat in the first round of the playoffs.

2022

Embiid wins the NBA scoring title after averaging 30.6 points per game during the regular season.

FRANCHISE HISTORY

Syracuse Nationals (1946–63),
Philadelphia 76ers (1963–)

NBA CHAMPIONSHIPS

1955, 1967, 1983

KEY PLAYERS

Charles Barkley (1984–92)
Wilt Chamberlain (1965–68)
Maurice Cheeks (1978–89)
Billy Cunningham (1965–72,
1974–75)
Joel Embiid (2014–)
Julius Erving (1976–87)
Hal Greer (1958–73)
Andre Iguodala (2004–12)
Allen Iverson (1996–2006,
2009–10)
Dolph Schayes (1948–64)
Ben Simmons (2016–21)
Chet Walker (1962–69)

KEY COACHES

Al Cervi (1948–57)
Billy Cunningham (1977–85)
Alex Hannum (1960–63,
1966–68)

HOME ARENAS

Onondaga County War
Memorial Coliseum
(1946–63)
Philadelphia Convention Hall
and Philadelphia Arena
(1963–67)
The Spectrum (1967–96)
Wells Fargo Center (1996–)
Formerly known as:
CoreStates Center
(1996–98)
First Union Center
(1998–2003)
Wachovia Center
(2003–10)

PLAYOFF REGULARS

The Nationals/76ers made the playoffs every year from 1947 to 1971. The 25-year streak would be the longest in NBA history, but the first three years came in the NBL. Officially, the streak is 22 seasons long, and it was tied by the San Antonio Spurs in 2019.

WHAT'S IN A NAME?

Darryl Dawkins often nicknamed his dunks. After one particular slam over Kansas City Kings forward Bill Robinzine, Dawkins dubbed it the "If-You-Ain't-Groovin', Best-Get-Movin', Chocolate-Thunder-Flyin', Robinzine-Cryin', Teeth-Shakin', Glass-Breakin', Rump-Roastin', Bun-Toastin', Glass-Still Flyin', Wham-Bam-I-Am-Jam."

MARATHON MEN

The Nationals and Boston Celtics played the longest playoff game in NBA history on March 21, 1953. The Celtics pulled out a 111–105 victory in four overtimes. Red Rocha and Paul Seymour of the Nats set an NBA record by playing 67 minutes each.

FUTURE CONSIDERATIONS

The draft pick that brought Charles Barkley to Philadelphia in 1984 was actually picked up in a trade six years earlier. The 76ers traded guard World B. Free to the San Diego Clippers in 1978 in exchange for the pick. When the deal happened, Barkley was a 15-year-old high school sophomore in Leeds, Alabama.

GLOSSARY

assist
A pass that leads directly to a basket.

double-double
Accumulating 10 or more of two certain statistics in a game.

draft
A system that allows teams to acquire new players coming into a league.

durable
Tough and long-lasting.

franchise
A sports organization, including the top-level team and all minor league affiliates.

homestand
A stretch of consecutive games played in a team's home city.

layup
A shot made from close to the basket; an easy shot.

meniscus
A piece of cartilage that sits behind the kneecap.

merged
Joined to form a new entity.

orbital bone
A bone that is part of the eye socket.

rookie
A professional athlete in his or her first year of competition.

tenacious
Unwilling to give up.

triple-double
Accumulating 10 or more of three certain statistics in a game.

BOOKS

Flynn, Brendan. *The NBA Encyclopedia for Kids*. Minneapolis, MN: Abdo Publishing, 2022.

Graves, Will. *NBA*. Minneapolis, MN: Abdo Publishing, 2021.

Mason, Tyler. *Ultimate NBA Road Trip*. Minneapolis, MN: Abdo Publishing, 2019.

ONLINE RESOURCES

To learn more about the Philadelphia 76ers, please visit **abdobooklinks.com** or scan this QR code. These links are routinely monitored and updated to provide the most current information available.

ABOUT THE AUTHOR

Patrick Donnelly is a freelance writer who lives in Minneapolis, Minnesota. He has covered the NBA for 20 years.